Difficult Conversations
a Mom Should Have
with Her Teenage Daughter

How To Talk About Love, Anger, Ego, Beauty and Sex

By

Biljana Ognenova

Difficult Conversations a Mom Should Have with Her Teenage Daughter

ISBN: 9781696540230

Warning and Disclaimer

Publisher contact

Skinny Bottle Publishing

books@skinnybottle.com

BILJANA OGNENOVA

Introduction

Why Should Anyone Be Telling You How to Talk to Your Child

All women are born with the same amount of eggs they are going to ever have in their lifetime.

While a daughter is in her mother's womb, she develops all eggs. If you think about it, this is what this literally means: the ovarian spark that brought you into existence was initiated in your grandma's womb. This is the biological line of female existence.

But one does not become a mom only by biology. One can become a mother by adoption or by surrogacy, and in many other magical and marvelous ways which establish the special bond between a nurturer and a protector.

There are many ways to mother a creation on the way to blossoming into a full human being. A father can become a mother. So many sisters and brothers have turned into mothers. Some aunts, uncles, grandmas, and grandpas do an amazing motherly job.

Even if the biological link to motherhood is predominant, most of us, male or female, can take the role of a mother. We can play it with gratitude and anxiety to the best of our abilities. Or, at least we can hope so!

If you're a mother plagued with challenges, this book will help you build your confidence for a number of important questions. Women will find the best use of the stories and examples told here. Yet, anyone who is confused about how to communicate with young women on their way to adulthood can recognize the value of some of the questions I am trying to shed a light on in this book.

The Most Difficult of All Difficult Conversations

The role of motherhood is one of the most judged roles in society. Many people think they know better than anyone else. Even the author of this book struggles with finding the delicate balance between offering a shared experience and downright patronizing.

That said; take anyone's opinion about motherhood with a (big) grain of salt. Despite the inability to stay away from emphasizing certain values, I definitely won't always know the right answers to your delicate questions. No one is better equipped to do your job as a mother than you are. However, we can agree that the struggle is real and help each other carry the burden.

On the other hand, moms are usually so invested in the mothering process that it's difficult for them to get out of the confinement of their own experience, thinking, and ideas. An objective outsider's opinion is definitely helpful.

"Why didn't I think of that perspective myself?", often goes through many mothers' minds when a trusted friend offers a pearl of original wisdom for solving a long-lasting.

And this is how we come to the first and the most difficult conversation you are going to have. Guess what? It's not with your teenage daughter! The most difficult conversation you're going to have is the one with yourself. Because many of the difficulties you're facing with your teenage daughter come from personal trials.

But boy, oh, boy, how easy would life get if we all just knew all answers to the most difficult questions? Therefore, whenever you meet with a difficult topic, take it slow and easy.

Create a safe container for your own feelings while you are cruising to a better understanding of how to make them simple. You can't make difficult conversations easy by force. It's a gentle ride.

We All Struggle with Sensitive Issues

Mothers and daughters are into some serious enmeshment. They are women and they are biologically connected. This makes it complicated for any of them to take a neutral stance and keep the emotions from reaching a boiling point, for better or for worse.

Thankfully, no one asks from you to adopt a 100% neutral role. The passionate investment of motherly love and continuous support make even the most difficult conversations fly away. That doesn't mean that other fosterers or nurturers won't ever feel the need to talk to teenagers about complicated stuff. If you've taken that role, at least for a while, you'd better get prepared to debate around sensitive and controversial issues.

Even more than life in general, raising teenagers is often a subject of controversy. Keep in mind that times change. In fact, times change faster than ever. What used to take place in twenty years is now happening in a period of five. Even if it is down to perception, radical changes squeeze in a shorter time frame as years go by.

Take into account the personal space of your daughter's world. Keep an eye on the life created in this moment of time and remember that your daughter is living a life of her own.

Chapter 1

Mothering and Smothering: An "S" that Makes Ripples of Difference

Even if you've won a gold medal for being the best mother of the century, you'll make it easier for you if you learn to step aside from the role of an overprotective mother. Some people use a pejorative word for that role. They call overprotective mothers control freaks.

Although no one can blame you if you turn into that during your child's adolescence (I wonder how many moms have a story to tell of a time when such controlling attitude saved their teenage daughter's immature ass), try and develop some distance from time to time.

Since it is not easy to get out of the enmeshed and instinctive motherly role, maybe this book can serve you as guidance. Think of these examples like having a helping hand from a mentor. The mentor is concerned about the

11

wellbeing of your daughter but is not hooked on the connection created by the umbilical cord and doesn't bear the responsibility of a full-time mom.

Don't Be Afraid of a Healthy Conflict

As a blessing or as a curse, the role of the mom includes conflict and resistance. You are witnessing the growth of a person whose direction is taking a life of its own.

Conflict is a good thing. It helps in developing critical thinking, nourishing independence, giving voice to personal needs and issues and standing up for yourself. A healthy conflict can turns daughters from "yes" women to persons who can differentiate between going with the flow and stepping into genuine independence even when there is no one to support them.

To moderate conflict and agreement, taking the perspective of a mentor is of immense help. Mothers can often get lost in their protective role and forget that they also play important roles in their own and in other people's lives. Moms are lovers, wives, managers, and friends, too. Above all, they need to enjoy in their own life instead of living the life of their daughter. This is often the biggest challenge during conflicts, difficult conversations, and difficult decisions.

I hope that you will sigh with relief at least a couple of times by the end of this book. Let's go and dive into making the conversations with teenage daughters as smooth, as easy and as flowing as possible.

The Tricky Question of Good and Bad Moms

Here is a question:

What kind of mother are you?

How long does it take you to think of a proper answer? Or of one that won't take half an hour to elaborate?

We can begin by setting two basic examples. A warning - they do color your possible answer with judgment and ethical conundrums.

Despite the fact that we like staying away from too much judgment, we can't just altogether dismiss it. We need it for setting boundaries. We need to be able to decide what's acceptable and what's not acceptable for us. And this is how we come to the archetypes of a "good" or a "bad" mom.

Picking one of these two categories is the most succinct answer one could give to the above question - what kind of mother are you?

While we all strive at being "good" mothers, most of us know better, at least when we are totally honest with ourselves. We know that we are sometimes "bad" mothers. Admitting the extent of the "badness" we create is a bit more challenging. We are either not ready or not aware.

Whenever I need to make a distinction between bad or good, I get inundated with the volume of bewildering half-truths. What really is good and bad motherhood?

Clearing up the ethical clouds from the grey skies of good and bad motherhood is an essential step you need to take to make those difficult talks with your daughter get by in a jiffy. It's challenging to talk about difficult subjects when you haven't figured out what's your take on it yourself!

Easier said than done. This ethical gauging process is relative and depends on the context.

So, let's speak of the relativity that influences moms to switch between these two labels. When do you choose what badge you put on your chest?

Is There a Picture-Perfect Mom?

Have you ever seen the show "Sex & the City"? If you are at all a follower of mainstream Hollywood series production, then you must have dedicated at least some time to one of its episodes.

Then, it won't be difficult for you to recognize the prototype of the "perfect" mother in Charlotte. Charlotte put a lot of pressure on herself because she wanted to be the perfect person. And how could a person be perfect if she doesn't behave at her best as a mom?

This perfect motherhood concept brought to the screen in "Sex and the City's" Charlotte has a lot to do with the archetype of the good mother set in Christianity. The immaculate female goddess concept is inherent to many religions, not only to Christianity. It still has a lot to do with the socially ingrained picture of the perfect mom in most women's heads.

If you were an avid fan of the series, then you probably remember the scene when Charlotte had presumably had a big failure in her role as a mother. Although her adopted

14

daughter Lily was not yet a teenager, but a toddler, it's easy to draw a parallel. The point is that Charlotte was all alone with Lily in her kitchen, there was no one else around her and she was her own worst judge.

As most children usually do, Lily was testing Charlotte's limits. Keeping her cool was close to being impossible. Many moms would snap out of it way before Charlotte lost her patience. At one point Charlotte couldn't handle it anymore. On the brink of losing it, she locked herself down in the kitchen niche and started weeping.

You see, Charlotte didn't want her daughter Lily to see her in her imperfection - sobbing uncontrollably. The benefits of Charlotte's behavior as a mom who is able to manage her own emotions without expecting the children to carry the load for her are remarkable. Yet I can't help but think that this incident had more to do with Charlotte's harsh judgment toward herself than with the impact on Lily if she had seen her mom in her imperfect self.

Trying to maintain this ideal image will make many conversations with your daughter difficult. Flowing with the full spectrum of emotions will help both you and your daughter turn into wholesome persons, thus creating a genuine irreplaceable bond. It's the age old-wisdom of leading by personal example. A mother who fully accepts herself will be able to do the same for her daughter.

"Three Billboards Outside Ebbing, Missouri" - a Hard Lesson in Acceptance

There are moms on film and there are real moms who are just like Charlotte. Then, there is a different type of mothers. Some mothers are not colored in pink personality traits, sprinkled with proper vocabulary and coming with a "Prim & Proper" maintenance guide. They are raw, indigestible, enraged and freed from sweet and tasty character spices. In parallel to the angelic goddess, mom lives the unapologetic and the disagreeable one.

If you are able to look into yourself for long enough, you will be able to see both types of mothers within you. Nosedive into a long and honest self-reflection, and you'd be able to see this different type of mom, the one pictured in the role of Mildred Hayes, the edgy main character in the critically acclaimed 2018 Oscar candidate "Three Billboards Outside Ebbing, Missouri".

The film raised some moral controversy on its own. That is not within the scope of interest of this book, though. Mildred, masterfully played by Frances McDormand, is not a hundred-percent likable character She is not up to Hollywood standards or to many people's picture of an ideal person.

What's important for this book is that she is far from a perfect mother. She swears, insults and quarrels. In her anger and violence, there isn't too much explanation about why she is the way she is.

(Warning of a spoiler alert - if you haven't watched the movie, skip to the next chapter.)

The tragic event that is the base of the story has a lot to do with the fight she pulls off with her angry and violent nature. It helps her fight against seemingly dreaded and mismatched opponents. She is totally unapologetic while taking justice into her own hands.

Before the tragic event, we see glimpses of Mildred's conversations with her daughter. In a nutshell, let's just say that she is the total opposite of Charlotte. She doesn't like hiding anything. Her language is rude, even cruel.

In contrast to Charlotte, who walks around her daughter on eggshells, Mildred yells and deals with her teenage daughter using a street language. Here is an illustration. Before the tragedy, Mildred tries to persuade her daughter to keep herself safe when going out. Her daughter is a tough nut herself. They get into a fight with an infamous end. The fight ends with Mildred saying to her daughter: "Well, I hope you get raped!" in her powerlessness to produce a different outcome with peaceful methods. She is infuriated because her daughter is not listening.

If you've seen the movie, then you know these harsh words have very little with what Mildred is truly like. The full scope of her fiery personality develops all the way until the end of the film. A large part of her behavior is fueled by the overwhelming love she has for her daughter.

Can you really put an easy label to Mildred? Is she a good or a bad mom?

Talking Like a Mentor: What does This Mean?

Any woman, including all mothers by biology or by role, have precious and life-saving gifts to offer to their teenage daughters, even when their self-belief is clouded in dark doubt.

Your own history as a woman carries stories that your daughter is just starting to discover. As a mother, you are often overburdened by the overprotective role.

"How can I act as a mentor, when I'm her mother?", you may ask. This question is full of truth many mothers share, but it also creates difficulties since it touches on many mothers' unhealed feminine wounds.

It's not easy to make the right choice between what is wrong and what is right when you need to explain sensitive topics such as changing bodies, sexuality and menstrual cycles and find the right course for guiding her through friendship and romance.

If you get out of your mom's head and adopt some objectivity to act more like a mentor, you can help your daughter thrive as a young woman in unprecedented ways. You can garner growth and heal wounds. You can offer your daughter the information, the guidance and the safety you missed when you were at her age.

Chapter 2

Moms Are for Life - Why the Teen Age, Then?

Motherhood doesn't stop once you raise your daughter to independence. The lifelong role stays. Yet when your daughter becomes a teenager, she is starting the process of turning from a child into a woman. She is learning to leave the safety of the family container and the support of grownups. At this point, she starts exploring and finding her core self.

This self will be largely shaped by the home values she had as a child and by her own choices and affinities as she grows up.

The birth is the time when a daughter has her umbilical cord cut to separate her from the physical body of her mom. Growing out of the teen age has more to do with cutting the soul cord. This symbolic gesture illustrates what it means for her to be able to grow into a woman and shape her own self-identity.

All periods of raising a daughter are important. But a teenage daughter will pass through the critical gates construed, chiseled and refurbished by puberty and sexuality. She will come in touch with the critical energy that will connect her to the multiple roles she can take in her life. If she wants to, she can become a creator, a mom, and a lover, using the transformative energy to learn how to shape her own personality around her true self. To make it fit within the context or within her close and more distant social world, your daughter will have to question the truths you have been telling her and the truth she is hearing from everyone else.

The Dragon Hidden in Each Girl before She Hits Puberty

Have you ever had a chance to talk to a 10-year old girl?

Before girls hit puberty they are the most confident people in the world. They have overcome the inevitable stresses of adopting basic life skills. They have learned to manage their place as a young person at school and family. They got a pretty good picture of what the world is about. Their talents and weaknesses have been tested. They know what are their strongest points. Pre-teen girls are still full of fresh personal content, free from socially-ingrained messages and ready to vigorously defend where they come from.

There is a small dragon hidden in any 10-year old girl. If you've run a debate with a girl around this age, you'd be scared by their rhetorics. They're invincible. Since they have a pretty good idea of what they are all about, pre-teen girls are in an advantageous age for picking up their future profession or purpose. Basically, they know what they are good at, what they enjoy in and how they can create a meaningful life for them out of this intuitive knowledge.

This is one of the difficult conversations you may need to have with your daughter - the one about her profession, work, purpose or life-work, as many love to call it. Before puberty, sexuality and complex emotions start hitting hard, girls' choices are more authentic. Let's leave this conversation take place in its due chapter.

At this point, discovering the framework of this particular age is more important.

Why Are Conversations With Teen Girls Difficult?

The hardest truths are those that we are trying to hide from ourselves. A hidden truth makes communication difficult. If we can be honest with ourselves, our communication will flow.

But this is not always easy. Our thoughts and opinions are fluid and under the strong impact of our subconscious.

If you are a woman you may not be a mother, but you are definitely a daughter. You've learned to shape the truth by stories and values accumulated in your own way of growing up. Usually, the women present in your life substantially influenced your thoughts and your behaviors.

Hey - no wonder this book is titled as it is!

Difficult things become easy when they are shared. That is one of the main purposes of this book: to share the problems of difficult conversations and thus ease the burden of the process.

Role Misfits?

By now you've probably figured out that a lot of the tone of this book is articulated by the values of womanhood. Womanhood is associated with gender. Now, that's one complicated subject to breach! After all, moms also have teenage sons. A mom can be a dad at the same time and a daughter might not even fit in the typical socially created gender role.

Like it or not, we are defined by society. For the purposes of this book, we will keep on the edges of the feminine archetype as interpreted or outlined in the mainstream female role. See, I'm not even sure that I've explained this subject well! I'm not a gender expert nor I am so aware of the appropriate vocabulary to address gender issues. I guess what I'm trying to say is that if you can't see yourself fit in the typical role of a mom who has a teenage daughter in a typical nuclear family, I still think that many of the points made in this book will apply to your situation.

Keep in mind that if you don't fit in the typical roles as described here, you can find value in the chapters as they touch on themes that make it difficult for us to communicate as humans. Some conversations are difficult, regardless of age, the relationship or the role the participants have taken!

Chapter 3

Finding Your Own Voice in Conversations

I have a relevant personal story. It's about haircuts. A favorite topic for moms. And for daughters!

From time to time, I have a habit to change my hairstyle. Not so long ago, I changed my brighter hazelnut into a darker, rigid style. I got the layers cut and the waves removed. I was very happy with the result. It reminded me of a similar style I've worn some ten years ago. My hair became shinier and bouncier. I felt like life was finding its way back into it.

It wasn't a big surprise for me to feel so good about it. The particular hairstyle was connected to a period in my life that awakens good memories. However, it was refreshing to hear the comments from my mom or my sister, as well as from my friends. Not one of the comments was the same! While my friend was so happy to see me abandon the previous hairstyle, my mom thought something completely else.

Everyone was trying to mold me into their preconceived idea of what they thought was the perfect hairstyle for me.

Just imagine how confusing this overwhelming response can get for a teenage girl if she starts listening to what everyone else has to say about her life choices. The preferred style or looks is the least of all possible problems, though it is not insignificant. There is bountiful information in the media on the looks checklist. The least a young woman needs is more options. In this view, there is a really slight difference between abundance, choice, and garbage.

When the authentic personal inner voice of a teenager gets polluted by voices from the environment, be it from close bonds or from media commercials, all that clutter becomes a huge burden which further complicates things.

A similar trivial real-life story comes from an exercise about body wellness I did a few years ago. This particular exercise was about weight loss. The girl who volunteered was asked to get into a middle of the circle, close her eyes and wait for the messages from the rest of the circle members. The moderator gave instructions to each participant by whispering them into their ears. No one in the group knew the messages other members got.

Oh, the poor girl! She just wanted to find the right diet to help her lose weight and thought this was going to be the outcome of this exercise. That's why she was so eager to volunteer (By the way, many thought that she shouldn't lose weight at all and, if you ask me, she looked excellent).

She hardly knew what was coming for her. After we got our messages, one by one, we were told to relentlessly spell the messages out to the girl, all at once. When she opened her eyes, she was bombed with thirty or forty different messages, some of which were a total opposite. Around forty people were yelling into her face. For example, I was instructed to tell her: "If you won't lose weight, you'll never get pregnant". Another girl a few spots down the circle was instructed to tell her: "If you won't put on weight, you'll never get pregnant".

When all these conflicting voices started all at once, all this girl could hear was an incessant babbling noise cut through with words and sentences from contradictory messages. We threw them at her with the force of self-righteous messengers, all of us convinced of the adequacy and the supremacy of the personal message.

That was one very clever moderator! I loved how this exercise turned into a reflection of the world is small. The messages ringing in that girl's ears are a lot like the countless messages we get from society, mostly from mainstream media.

The girl in the middle of the circle listened for a while and then just put her palms on her ears yelling - "Stop!" Then she left the circle stuttering "No, no, no." In the end, she burst out laughing understanding the ridiculousness of her situation. She got the message, although it was not what she expected to hear at the beginning.

Apart from her own, your daughter will have to listen to many other voices. Try not making make your own as forceful as one of the thousands. If you force conversations at a time when girls are in a mess of emotions and conflicting opinions you will make any conversation more difficult than it is, regardless of the topic. I guess that if we want to make a rule out if this, Rule #1 for easier conversations would be to let all participants be able to find, shape and use their own voice.

Chapter 4

Don't Exasperate - Illuminate

(Guiding Framework on What Can Make Topics Difficult)

What makes a conversation with your teenage daughter difficult? We can safely assume that it's not for the same reasons that create problems in conversations you take on with a boss who is a difficult person. Most likely, your daughter is not a jackass all the time, although I'm sure she can be, from time to time!

Here are a few possible factors that can make it hard for you to spill the right words out about a particular topic.

Confusion

Confusion is about having a lot of questions about a topic, and not knowing the answers to many of them. You listen to experts, talk to your friends and follow social media. Nobody seems to agree with the answers in total. If no one knows the right answers or so many people think they do, how are you going to give them to your daughter as guidance when she is thirsty for discovering her life's truth?

Taboo

Taboo topics are painted by group ethics. That doesn't necessarily mean that widely acknowledged taboo topics will be taboo for you, too. Some topics may be a personal taboo only for you, and that's all right. You don't need to have all your answers neatly packed all the time.

Controversy

Taboo and controversy go hand-in-hand. The difference is that taboos are like controversy hidden in plain sight. Controversy is like a taboo brought on the table to be dissected to pieces. Controversial topics are infused with many personal and general truths, which can make conversations even more difficult.

Shame

Shame is the most underestimated and the least explored emotion. The society is significantly shaped by the amount of shame we feel in social interaction. It's one of the most delicate aspects of a difficult conversation since it tells us how we deal with the wrong and the right in a personal space while being socially empathetic at the same time.

29

Honesty

When talking to your teenage daughter, honesty is really not the best policy under all circumstances. Most mothers struggle with the level of honesty they need to invest in a conversation. Honest conversations are wrapped in sensitivity. It's fine to adopt gradual honesty and keep some parts of the truth to yourself until you feel comfortable enough to share them.

We all know that it's not enough to set a bullet list of five subjects and hope that we have found the key to making all conversations less difficult. However, if you keep the above topics in your awareness when you hit a brick wall with your daughter, they can be used as an appropriate ointment to massage it in the most painful spots, both for you and for your daughter.

Chapter 5

How to Talk About Love

Children love because they are loved. Adults love because they - love. Immature love is about loving someone because of a need. Mature love is about needing someone because of loving them. Being awestruck is not proof of the strength of love, it is merely proof of the loneliness that preceded it.

Most people believe that love depends on the object, and not on their personal capacity to love. This belief results in the thinking that loving no one else but one person, is proof of the strength of their love.

Love focused on an object is a delusion. This situation is very similar to a painter who learns painting and claims that in order to start painting the most wonderful art; all he needs to do is find the right landscape. Then the painting will happen by itself. If you truly love someone, you will find love for all people, the whole world and the whole life.

If I say "I love you" to someone, I have to be able to include that entire person in the love. Real love is about loving the world and loving yourself thanks to the beloved other. Wholesome love includes self-love, as well as loving others. Instead of losing yourself, love should help you find yourself in another person.

Falling in love is not the paramount love experience. It's the beginning of love; only a possibility to acquire loving skills. People usually think love is some sort of mysterious experience of mutual affinity between two people and that the magical event takes place by itself. In fact, loneliness and sexual desire make falling in love an easy experience. There is nothing mysterious about it. It goes away as quickly as it came. There is no loving by accident. Your capability to love electrifies another's love; in the same way that showing interest makes another person interesting. It's very important to be capable of being alone. It's a prerequisite for love.

If you don't know how to speak to your daughter about love, this is because there is a profound crisis in the world. We are unable to love since we are too distracted by greed, ignorance, and pursuit of power. We are in need of an evolutionary and transformative love that will emerge to help the loving partners maintain a deep reverence and devotion to the other. Again, if you can't master being alone, work on that before you do everything else. You should be your own best company before you can offer or recognize that companionship in another. Understand that love is not a power play and that the other person's dignity is sacred. Love like you are in a meditative state with the beloved person.

Relationships are not based on Hollywood sentimentality. People in love come with their shadows. Mature love is about presence in the shadow space. Forget about perfect personalities without shadows. Each person comes with wounds. Love is all about watching over the shadow while being aware that you are not manipulated or doing the same in return.

Love always changes. A loving relationship is not only created for the pleasure of the persons in it. It includes a conscious reverence for the planet and the world around us. It needs to be able to transform a world full of distraction, greed and stop the mouse race for power. Love is creation and divinity which are kept under the same roof. If you believe in God, this is where you'll see his reflection. If you don't, this is where you'll see a reflection of yourself. Power and love are not the best of friends.

To observe the polarized world we live in and get a basic picture of what it means to have a shadow, you can try talking to your daughter by using the language of the Jungian feminine and masculine archetypes. All people come with both parts inside. If you are a woman who is not aware that you possess the masculine aspect within, you will be forever searching for it to find it in men. If you are a man who is unconscious about the feminine part, you will be always searching for it in women. Once you recognize and accept the fact that you are both of these archetypes, and incorporate both parts in your own self, you'll stop the quest to find the perfect counterpart in another. You won't stick to it when you miss it and hate it when it becomes too much.

Your soul has no gender. This dynamic quest to find the polar part in another is what many relationships are based on. It's exciting and attractive, like the candle's flame for a moth. A wholesome love experience is about understanding that both men and women are human and that's where you should take off.

Love within Boundaries: How To Create Comfortable Distances

Do you get too close to your daughter and drown her with worry, wondering why she gets irritated?

We tend to do that.

Let's see how this works in relationship with your husband or partner. Lie close to him, with your face next to his and your bodies in a tight embrace.

How long can you lie like that? After a while, you'd want to get out and breathe some fresh air. Do you feel ashamed because of that feeling?

Mothers often do this with daughters, metaphorically breathing into their faces and not giving them a break. We do the same in all relationships, creating unhealthy distances.

Everyone needs some personal space. Some require a huge circle, while others need just a minimal breathing space. You need your space, too, even if you haven't figured out that already.

Harming a personal space and even the smallest trespassing can be harmful. A single word, one insult or a small humiliation can break another person's integrity. This is why it is important to talk to your daughter about respecting personal boundaries. Without them, healthy loving relationships are impossible.

If it's difficult to identify what's a personal boundary or what's the desired distance between herself and other people, let the following questions help her:

"Is this a question I'm comfortable with? Does it lack tactfulness?"

"Am I ready to carry this pain and sadness that is being poured down on me?"

"Did I ask for this advice?"

"Is this a critique I am ready to accept? Who does it come from?"

"Do I really need to do what I'm asked to do?"

"Am I doing this for someone else because of a sense of guilt or shame?"

"Am I being asked to adopt another person's worldview, goals, and objectives and abandon my own?"

"Am I being pressured because of my attitudes and opinions?"

"Am I getting a promise of love in exchange for doing something uncomfortable?"

"Am I letting another do what they want because I'm silent? Is this a silent agreement?"

"Do I unconsciously help other people break my boundaries?"

"Have I left an open door to my soul?"

The answers to the above questions give plenty of food for thought about who we are letting into our personal world.

Why do we do that? There are simple and not so simple reasons behind this practice, composed of a series of behaviors with one thing in common: the inability to develop a healthy distance between ourselves and the others.

We can't say no and we don't listen to our hearts. Trying to be good for everyone, avoiding mistakes, and striving to achieve perfection are key ingredients that get thrown into the mix. Keeping emotions in check, we avoid upsetting people. To achieve some result, we are ready to go through torture until we get there. We rape our bodies and souls to get money, respect, recognition, approval or love. Focusing on the bad, we don't notice the good stuff and forget about being grateful for all that we already have.

A thousand small and big personal betrayals become a part of our life. By betraying ourselves we just help the trespassers hurt our integrity. We become like a fragile vase placed at the end of a table that gets shattered into small pieces when a reckless bystander moves by it.

In fact, we have allowed for that to happen. Is that passer-by to blame for the damage? Not really - the person was just minding his or her own business, and the boundary of the vase got in his way.

The metaphorical vase should be our greatest treasure. Instead of putting it in a safe drawer or a large closet and locking it down, we keep it out into the open. Afterward, it's all about thinking hard of who is our key holder; everyone should not be let in. Instead of being vocal about our boundaries, we let others in and let them wreak havoc while we keep a smile on our faces. We treat our soul, the vase, as dross that can be exchanged in a thrift shop for a cheap fee.

How can your daughter change all this? First, by starting to work on the relationship toward herself - living without force and authoritarianism, and supporting and believing in herself, even when no one else does. A daughter who knows how to set clear boundaries can take care of her soul and her body. She communicates only when she wants to, listens to herself and maintains her resources well replenished.

If she is in a relationship that causes pain, let her take a step back and maintain a safe distance. Staying away from the issue will help her live through the unpleasant emotions and the painful experience. She can shorten the distance and close the gap only when she wants to. This is the strongest recipe for the success of any loving relationship.

By the way, have your tired this yourself? Go for it, give yourself permission to do so!

At the same time, think about it from the other person's perspective: how often do you break someone's integrity trying to get too close? Is this perhaps the reason why all your conflicts start?

Boundaries and Trauma - Taking a Close Person's Trauma as Your Own

Hearing about someone's sad or difficult story can create trauma in your own nervous system. Although it's not the same as living through it personally, it still hurts, especially if you are closely related to the person. That's just how the nervous system works. Your nervous system gets in tune with the other person's and you both suffer.

It's important to talk to your daughter about this. She should be able to understand that close emotional connections share the suffering and the trauma. She may have heard that nurses in medical care take on the trauma of the patients that they are responsible for.

The same happens with close family and partners. While trauma doesn't necessarily make you a bad person, you may turn out to look like that on the outside; at least that's what you'll look like to your friends and family when you start acting irrationally or get burnout and totally collapse.

Survival mechanisms can make your daughter act irresponsibly and without compassion. Tell her to stop and ask her to recognize what is happening and to take some time off to process the suffering.

Setting boundaries in traumatic experiences is extremely important for a young woman to be able to support herself and the people she loves at the same time and with appropriate measures.

Sharing Happiness and Boundaries

You may think this is weird, but respecting boundaries also includes sharing happiness. Overwhelmed by happiness, we can't wait to share our positive energy. If there is joy in life, then we should share it with others, isn't that the truth? If it's too big, we feel like we want to share it with the whole world.

When sharing our joyful experiences, we expect a positive response from our communication partners. We are hoping for an encouraging and an inspired response. We wouldn't be happy with another type of reaction now, would we? If someone doesn't react as we expect them to, we can get confused, even downright furious. Our friends should be happy for us, shouldn't they? It's either their duty or they are not our friends.

Ah, well, our blind egoism forgets that we shouldn't think only about ourselves but about others, too. Maybe it's better to first check what's going on with the other person? Maybe now it's not the time to share what we intended to share? Can we cause someone's envy?

A friend of mine went on an expensive holiday. When I asked her about her impressions, she told me it was nothing special. "Well", I said in my head, "Good answer, that's the mantra of rich and intelligent people". They are aware of the envy they can cause and they make sure they stop doing that. It's a human and polite way of dealing with people who don't always have access to the same resources you do.

When someone asks about the cost of the shoes you have just bought, perhaps it's good to pause for a while and say - "I don't remember" or "They were a gift", or something like that. It's rude to brag about your own children to a couple that cannot have them. It's ridiculous to bask in detailed descriptions about the mansion you own to a person that is struggling with basic rent arrangements.

The biggest problem is typically what we think of ourselves, and not of others. We don't like being sensitive about another's dignity. Even if that is one of the most joyful events in our lives, we should think about how much we tell others, and how much we tell to random allies.

This is a common problem for modern people. They get ecstatic when something good happens and shaken when something bad happens to them. When emotions go wild, they need a valve to let them out. The end result is living in a constant state of emotional burps and expecting from the close ones to handle and understand such behavior.

Talk to your daughter about the relative meaning and significance of all experiences. A spiritually balanced person understands that everything in the world changes so fast that we really can't tell if what happened to us was a good or a bad experience.

We don't know what's behind the curve. Our vision reaches the edge of our awareness and encompasses the situation that just happened to us. We shouldn't pour the bucket of our stories over the heads of our closest and more distant people.

Developing listening skills is one of the best skills your daughter can train. Anyone can talk about themselves. Personal development often means including the happiness of others into our own.

Throwing a party for a person in mourning is not the best possible advice at all times. Sometimes, our greatest joy is another person's greatest sorrow. It doesn't always mean that the other person is evil or envious, but it can mean that we've been insensitive and impolite.

Share happiness with a few people who are happy to accept your joy. Do this selectively and carefully.

Chapter 6

How to Talk About Healthy Egoism

How will your daughter know where is the end of her needs and where is the beginning of the needs of other people? Where is the boundary of healthy egoism?

Teaching young women to be empathetic and compassionate is like skinning them alive. As a general rule, empathy is a sign of a developed and sensitive personality. But there is also an uncontrolled empathy toward the whole world, including the living and the artificial, the imaginary and the real worlds. Metaphorically, this is a world without skin or without a backbone.

Why do we call this process skinning alive? Because it describes a personal world without boundaries. The skin is the boundary where your body ends and the outside world begins. This membrane translates symbolically to your personality and your sense of self.

We set detrimental examples of unhealthy egoism even when the girls are very young and continue to do so as girls grow up:

"Look, Teddy Bear fell, it hurts him."

"Elisabeth is now crying because of you."

"Mommy feels bad because of you."

"No one wants to hang out with such a bad girl."

"You should call James; he was the one who got hurt."

"He is not a bad guy. Maybe he is yelling at you because he has problems."

Slowly, your daughter will start thinking about everyone else first and put herself last.

Indeed, why should anyone think about themselves, when they can think about others? This is so noble!

Being generous and noble is appreciated in theory, but works poorly in practice.

Who appreciates nobility? When people encounter very noble and giving persons, they tend to think more about personal interests. This unhealthy empathy often creates the equally harmful dynamics of taking too much of what's on offer by the givers. Somehow, you are never enough for others. You can hand over your heart on a silver tray and it will get ripped apart!

It's extremely difficult to learn self-care and self-protection when the emotions have grown into habitual skeletal patterns in our bodies. It's like holding the whole world on your shoulders. The situation stays the same for a long time, without any faith or clue of what to do and how to change it. When you become aware of this, you only know that you need to save yourself from the uncontrolled empathy, while there is still time. When your daughter is a teenager, she has more time to build healthier patterns.

When you talk to our daughter about selfishness, try to get rid of the socially negative overtone. How about letting her start examining the motives behind her empathetic behavior? You can suggest that she starts asking herself questions like these:

"What do I really feel?"

"Do I act like this because this is reasonable or because I want to be praised for my unselfishness and generosity?

"Do I avoid discussing and negotiating the issue because I'm afraid that I will hurt the person or because there is a point in arguing with this person?"

"Where does the healthy egoism end and the unhealthy begin?"

"Can I want too much now if I've been told that I wanted too much since I was a child?"

"What is the truth? Why I don't understand anything?"

Are these possible answers to the above questions?

"...Because I've never been taught to stop listening to everybody else and start listening to myself... To start searching for my own truth instead of accepting someone else's. I'm still learning."

But you see, this is not only one girl's problem. This is the problem of all women who've been violently scraped from their most important protection to become easier prey.

If you are unclear about what it means to be a healthy egoist, there is a strong female Buddhist voice that can help you get and set the basics. It is about suffering from 'idiot compassion'. The similar notion has been weaved throughout the pages of this book, but Pema Chodron put a really nice label on it.

Idiot compassion is about showing kindness to others even when the situation deserves a different response. Dostoevsky has a +600-page novel on the topic carrying a stunningly auspicious name - "The Idiot". If you don't have the time to read Dostoevsky's humongous writings, keep Pema's message close to heart to share it with your daughter.

The compassion that is harmful to us and that we apply only for the reason to protect our good image of a nice person is called idiot compassion. Healing yourself from the disease is done - again, by setting clear boundaries. This is the kindest thing we can do for ourselves and for the other person from the relationship in question. It's not okay to keep your heart open and let others walk all over it, just because you don't want to see it harden. Simply put, your compassion should always include yourself, as well as the others.

Chapter 7

How to Talk About Anger

Have you ever told your daughter that it is fine to be angry?

Anger is a powerful emotion, an action instigator and a great teacher of our needs. When a girl hears the message that being angry is unacceptable, she ditches a big part of herself. She is failing to use it as a guide toward knowing what's right and what's wrong for her.

Girls usually learn to dismiss and diffuse their anger. That's the worst that can happen to the powerful emotion. It becomes so lukewarm and relative, that girls lose the ability to feel it in their bodies, in turn understanding it better.

You've probably come across your angry girl when she was very young because small children weather with anger much better than teenagers. The wheels of social

47

acceptance are powered by the denial of anger. As we grow up, we are told that anger doesn't bode well for our relationships and that it's preferable to suppress it.

In case you've never talked to your daughter about anger, the teen age may offer a perfect opportunity to do it. And no, not everything is about hormones, anger included. More often than not, hormones are just a vehicle of genuine needs.

How can you help your daughter to understand anger better?

There is definitely a lot you can learn about your own and your daughter's anger only by observing her. But, here are some questions you can use to help her identify anger:

"Are you red, flushed or shaking?"

"Do you clench your jaws, especially at night?"

"Do you break out in sweat or in hives?"

"Do you feel like crying for no reason?"

"Why do you feel like laughing during difficult conversations"?

The simplest thing to do is to ascribe these behaviors to hormones. Making them inconsequential or attributing them to a development phase doesn't help your daughter in finding her own voice. At this point, it's worth thinking of a mom who was once only a daughter - you!

For many women, misunderstanding and withholding anger is a phase that never ends. This is an important message to share with you teenage daughter. Teach her to recognize her anger and believe that she has the right to express it without being afraid or at risk for speaking her truth.

All children, and daughters, in particular, are taught to be sociable, polite and agreeable. Many mothers do this unconsciously, setting a model that's not always productive. When you dismiss your anger, you dismiss your needs.

If you've been portraying this behavior and ask your daughter to do the same, it's no wonder so many conversations between the two of you feel so difficult!

A mother and a daughter with unmet needs in a circle of anger and love is a wild mix. Suffocating the anger in your body makes you more susceptible to autoimmune diseases. In less severe cases, living without expressing anger becomes a lifelong battle with stress, anxiety, and depression that transfers from the teen age long into the autumn of life.

If you tether on anger for too long and don't understand it well, it will be difficult to speak to your daughter about it. Anger that has been malnourished turns into resentment. When anger and resentment come together, a deeper truth hides behind the difficult feelings.

Your needs are unmet. You defend and close your heart. You have expectations about what should be happening. Expectations breed judgment, assign quilt and throw responsibility into the hand of other people. Whenever you find yourself wrapped in anger and resentment, it's wise to see what you're missing. What are the messages you are telling to yourself?

"What is it that I need?"

"Why is this so important to me?"

"Why is this making me so angry?"

Is there a truth in your answers? Are they only assumptions? This approach will broaden your perspective by suggesting alternative possible truths about the situation you find yourself in.

There isn't a lot of space for vulnerable feelings when we are into the anger. Anger has a lot of thinking in it. If you let go of the thoughts that you use to describe the anger, you'd be left with the feelings and the needs around them. Anger is the perfect indicator of what you miss in your life, so this is again a perfect tool to get familiar with them. Take ownership of your needs by recognizing and acknowledging them.

Here is a question for you: How does your daughter make you angry?

There are usually deeper feelings at the core of angry people. The typical culprits are fear and sadness. When you truly feel and express these feelings, it's easier to communicate the needs to the people around you.

Lead by example. You can talk about anger all that you want, but unless you demonstrate the behavior, you're unconsciously setting up an unhealthy pattern.

Talking about anger requires sitting still and approaching the other from a place of connection so that the other person is able to hear you. It doesn't have to do a lot with Mildred's profanity!

(There is an important point I would like to make here - despite her unpopular bearing, I am in deep awe of Mildred's character, both as a mother and as a woman. She is definitely an amazing person in many ways and there is plenty we can learn from her.)

This is a book about mothers and daughters. Although it's fine to keep it that way (it's the book topic, after all) that leaves us with the result of losing some of the father's wisdom if we choose to keep it absolutely that way.

Fathers can play an amazing role in the way their teenage daughters deal with anger. Therefore, it is a shame to miss out on a real-life example from a father who is helping his very young daughter cope well with her anger. In the end, both mothers and fathers are parents, and most aspects of their roles are shared.

I've never seen anything like this video.

https://www.facebook.com/JungleVT/videos/2002016979940134/

It is the best close-up of what it means to talk about anger in an awesome way. The video went viral on Facebook, fully deserving of its popularity. If you haven't watched it, don't miss it! We can all learn from this dad and the example he set for his little daughter. Yes, he is not a mom; and, yes, she is not a teenager, but he masters a difficult conversation about anger with aplomb. He deserves a "Be like This Dad" meme! When you watch it, pay attention to how he respects his daughter's boundaries. The little girl sets a boundary about her tolerance to his jokes. He agrees not to cross it. It's amazing to watch them in all their father-daughter awesomeness, the respectful communication and the 'anger floating' approach he advocates. He describes anger as a motivator, something that should be felt and then let it go away.

Anger is powerful, but we must learn to let it go at some point.

Chapter 8

Life Work and Purpose in the Fabric of Nature and Society

Why Earth is Your Home

Nature is your daughter's home. Women and nature have an unbreakable bond created on a spirit level. The wild nature of women is a synonym for the pure instinctive energy of the natural world. With the split of urbanization, we've moved away from our natural home.

Don't forget to tell your daughter that she was created in the womb of her mom, just as her home was created in the Earth's womb. Help her imagine the Earth as the mother of all. Raising an ecologically conscious child is a benefit that gets woven in the wholesome web of life by thoughtfully using and growing the resources we have to sustain ourselves and the people we love for a long way to come.

The core of nature in every human being is as ancient as humanity itself. Although the exciting technology times we live in create a cultural break from nature, there is now a backlash to revise our relationship with nature. We begin to embrace indigenous wisdom and start developing a balanced relationship with nature as the next step in our evolution.

Contemporary lives should not be shaped by consumerism. Why is this conversation important to have with your teenage girl? Right about the age girls hit puberty, the natural children's untamed nature starts getting strongly affected by the social norms. The need to be liked, the hormones and the interest in relationships are influenced by the social fabric. The society transfers to the little girls' wild nature with the possibility of distorting their deep intuitive voice.

The Helping Hand of Nature

When a young woman starts disconnecting from her internal voice, she starts making decisions which are not her own. No wonder so many girls change their worldview at the brink of puberty and start going into wrong professional directions!

Keeping in tune with nature includes three things: the nature of the planet as we know it, the nature of the ancestry transferred through our mom's womb and our true individual nature. It's not easy to balance all natures, but it can be grounding, connecting and purposeful for a young woman to find her place in this world and create or choose her life work, purpose, profession, and career.

Messages for Finding a Place and Purpose in the World

Stay away from small talk and bad company. What is a bad company? Let's just say that a bad company is made of zombie people. Zombie people are those whose soul is dead, who don't discuss, but jabber; people who don't think, but express widely-accepted opinions.

When people don't understand your behavior, they try to boss you around and control you, trying to tell you how to live your life. If they're offended by your freedom or irrationality, leave them be. It's their problem which is hidden behind the need for control. Don't ever be indifferent toward yourself. Your most important life task is to realize your potential. Invest most of your efforts in yourself.

Unless the act hurts or causes pain to another, you don't need to explain or justify anything to anybody. So many lives have been destroyed by explanations made in order to gain someone's understanding or approval. A free young woman has a vow to explain only to herself, and to a very few chosen ones who have the right to ask for that.

Be a person for yourself. This self-love is neither self-denial nor narcissism. It's a humanistic idea lead by the idea for self-affirmation. The meaning of life is the one we give it by living a creative and fruitful purpose while unveiling our best talents and powers to the world.

This message will help your daughter live spontaneously, free from an automatic coercive way of doing things, making her own sense of life and its purpose. There is no guarantee of happiness. Happiness is a personal accomplishment of your gifts. There is a trick behind this freedom of choice - you may think you are living for yourself when, in fact, you are living for everyone else.

Make the right choices, above all, make your own choices. You don't want to live in the shadow of the choices you haven't made, carrying work as a burden and as a means for protection and safety. Being alive is a dynamic process and the purpose of living has a lot to do with uncovering one's potential.

Experiencing compassion is about living the same experience as the other person and becoming one in the process. All knowledge about the others is limited by our compassionate ability to experience the world of another. A close person cannot be saved by making a choice for them. You can give hints with love and truth. Giving unwanted and unneeded alternatives, sentimentality and illusion are not necessary. Sorrow, sadness, and joy are equal parts of life. Suppressing them is impossible. Tragedies happen - live through them.

Chapter 9

How to Nurture Creativity with Rest

Do you think your daughter spends too much time on her iPad?

Silence is the space of intense creative potential. The womb is silent. The birth space of those 'a-ha' moments in which authors think of an original plot twist, managers solve a problem and scientists find the answer to a theory that has long plagued them is totally quiet.

In the digital age, we are missing the void of sacred quiet spaces. We drive connected cars and live in automated homes. We read books on electronic devices before we go to bed. We like having the whole world of information at the tip of our fingers. If we are not plugged in, we think we are missing something. Slowly but surely, we are getting used to having the dopamine dose that comes from the constant information feed.

57

How does this happen?

If this is worrying for you, you understand the importance of downtime, me-time or quiet-time. Downtime is a chance to stay in an uninterrupted quiet space where imagination thrives and where new seeds of creativity are born. We need to get disconnected from time to time, digest all that information flow and give space for something new to come into existence.

So, how can you talk to your daughter about this topic when she seems like she was born with the smartphone glued to her fingers?

Above all, we need to understand that we crave constant information stimulation because staying calm in empty spaces is scary. When there is nothing to distract us, we are alone and in touch with our true deepest self. Our quiet core selves are wrapped in existential loneliness, fear, and anxiety that creep in if there is nothing else to fill their place. This is why so many people can't spend a minute without some sort of engagement. Now you probably get an idea of why social networks are so popular!

The need for connection is in human nature. It stands high in the human hierarchy of needs. We are recognized by others. We grow with physical contact. Our self-confidence is a product of interaction with others. True intimate connections are the food for the soul and the body.

So, has it come now to digital spaces to provide the craved connection? Can thousand meaningless 'loves', 'likes' or 'wows' provide what we are looking for? Is your photo the real you?

Of course not! But that virtual space has somehow turned into a tool for checking the verity of our own existence. We need the significance of these distractions to reassure ourselves that we matter and that we are valuable.

Then, you may think, with all this awareness, there must be a way to talk to my daughter about sacred spaces. How do I help both of us fight for an uninterrupted me-time without distractions?

Celebrate weekends and holidays. People didn't invent and maintain rituals around holidays for nothing. If we don't set calendar dates to remind us of the so much needed downtime, we forget about it. We fall into the trap of super-productivity and use our free time to get more distracted and get more work done.

Don't work on holidays. How about setting some time for you each week to spend it by yourself? What about talking to your daughter to remember that she is worthy enough without constant engagement and that she doesn't have to be at an all-time-high to keep up with the ridiculous self-imposed distraction pace?

Who knows, by setting an unpopular example, she may overturn a few 'distraction addicts' to downtime aficionados.

Let her welcome silence as a daily practice and leave some time for deep thoughts. If your daughter doesn't take the time to set the discipline for herself (with your support) no one else will do it for her. Countless information sources are fighting to get her attention, and it has never been easier for teenagers to click the baits.

How about thinking of unplugging the Wi-Fi for an hour a day and dedicating it to deep presence? That said, mothers are sometimes unaware that their daughters live in a totally different era. Being online for longer periods of the day is not unusual. This is why it's important to think about the perspective your daughter might have about this.

While setting some control can be great, overstepping the boundaries of a teenager who is finding her own voice in this world can easily turn her mom into a control freak. The daily ritual can be supported by meditation practice, but I'd yet want to meet more teenage girls who are excited by long-term benefits of meditation! As a replacement, sleeping works wonders - only if it would have been so easy for teenagers to relax and get there during the day!

All that anxiety and fear that shows up during times of quiet presence is smoothed up by the superfluous information distraction. When we embrace our insecurities and understand that plugging into the information matrix relieves them, spending some time alone turns into a treasury.

It is exactly in the deep space of alone time, which is accompanied by conscious and unconscious fears, that creative people do some of their best work. Thanks to existential craziness, we see a world full of beautiful art. This is how downtime can become your daughter's friend. Staying in it is like an investment in a limitless pool of creativity.

Talk to your daughter about relaxation. Teach her to stay away from jumping to conclusions and rushing into decisions. Speed will guide her in familiar ways. Slow-motion is about the sacredness of silence.

Each minute, the world around us is trying to speed us up, asking us to be bigger, bolder and faster. Is this really necessary? Can we stay undistracted for a few minutes without plans and intentions?

When your daughter allows herself to stop the relentless chase for a while, she starts to develop a lifelong habit of optimal functioning. Even if it doesn't impact her significantly during her teenage years, she will get in touch with the amazing ideas that come only during shower-time or while falling asleep at night. This time will become a miniature sacred space to get in touch with the most authentic self.

Chapter 10

How to Talk About Beauty

At the moment of birth, we don't really know what beauty is. It takes several months to develop the functions necessary to be able to recognize the features on other people's face. This is usually our mom. At first, we recognize the smell, since this was the famous smell we got used to while we were in the womb.

It's just expected that the most beautiful person in a small baby's life should be its mom! The small baby is not yet shaped by the social standards of beauty.

Although you definitely don't remember what it was like to be an infant, you must remember a later point in your life when you thought that your mom was the most beautiful person in the world. Toddlers and small children have a tendency to do that. They think that their moms are the most beautiful creatures simply because they get accustomed to and familiar with their facial features. The loving face becomes the beautiful face.

This is the first definition of beauty that girls adopt during life. However, this definition almost never stays the same. Various social influences make their impact. Sometimes, as women, we are more at liberty to adopt a personal view of beauty, but more often than not, we digest the value food placed on our plates by social factors.

The original stance of a small child (what is close is also beautiful) gets transformed into a distorted view of beauty heavily burdened by meeting social criteria.

Aesthetics is a deep human need. It's ridiculous to deny that beauty is important. We are ravenous for beauty in all shapes. If we didn't appreciate beauty, no artist would ever be able to imagine and produce masterpieces we know that exist and deeply admire. In art creation, beauty gets modeled from a vital force that carries the instinctive passion for life. In a nutshell, beauty is an affirmation of life.

So, what messages would you like to give to your daughter about beauty?

Should you let her experience the sense of beauty you have about the world and make her reflect your own opinion? How can you connect that to the notion that beauty is a deep personal need?

Is there a difference in the definitions of beauty in general and in art aesthetics? Can you say that beauty is not important? Is it something harmful or something ecstatic?

If you don't want your daughter to mirror your opinion, you may choose to avoid discussing beauty. Adopting this choice (a legitimate one!) leaves more space for taking other people's views and absorbing what the general media has to say on the subject. She may not learn the difference between a beautiful and an ugly person, which makes defining beauty even more complex.

Most moms are torn between beauty's double standards for young women. None of them wants to make beauty totally useless, unimportant or negative. In contrast, not all mothers want to make beauty something that is worth obsessing over.

Would you want to tell your daughter that she is beautiful non-stop so that she becomes obsessed with it? How about the opposite question - would you tell your daughter that she is not beautiful?

You don't need to share the answers to the above questions with your daughter. If you have to choose a consummate message, make it about the wholeness of a person. Hopefully, most of you will agree that talking about beauty in all that it encompasses - emotional, spiritual, physical and mental aspects - is a healthy message. Each of these aspects deserves to be recognized and valued. Talking about all types of beauty is a much better option than avoiding it or painting it with negative colors.

Beauty includes wisdom, cleverness, strength, and capabilities. Can you imagine a teenage girl that grows confident with a rainbow of positive messages about how beautiful she is in all her parts?

Conflicting messages are all over the place. Physical beauty is the most discussed and a seriously controversial issue, not only for women but also in general. Luckily, we are witnessing a new era when the world is awakening to a new type of beauty. Beauty is no longer only about perfectly symmetrical eyes, but also about a crooked nose, a sagging belly, and weirdly proportioned bodies. A beautiful person is not only the one that resembles an angel. Some beautiful women have many devilish physical and personality traits!

We are collectively awestruck by beauty and this part of our nature as women shouldn't be denied. Admiring beauty brings us closer to our survival instincts and to a purposeful life.

Beauty is about love, growth, joyfulness, sexuality, and ecstasy. It should be celebrated in all its glory and in all its appearances - as art and intellect, and as power and humility. Then we just might ignite the charge each young woman carries as an idea to transform the socially twisted beliefs about beauty that include meeting criteria which change as times go by.

Your daughter is the most beautiful when she is - herself.

Chapter 11

What Does it Mean to Be Attractive

Why is being attractive an important topic for your teenage daughter? And why would a conversation around it be difficult?

Attraction can be so many different things to different people. As a general rule, when teenage girls talk about being attractive, they think of physical attraction. And who can blame them? Physical attraction is amazing, but when it's the only aspect of attraction because most grownups use the same vocabulary to transfer the attraction message, then teenage girls learn that attraction and seduction are one and the same thing.

To clarify where I'm coming from here, let me give you an example. Attraction is about radiance, and seduction is about manipulation. Sure, both are sometimes necessary. However, when we radiate, we are genuinely in resonance with the things and the people that are good for us. Likewise, we are good for them.

To become attractive, empathy for our environment is a key, but not the only ingredient. We need to learn to enjoy our own presence.

Talk to your daughter about keeping her identity. Being attractive is about our truest identity, which is free from impersonation and shapeshifting into other people's identities. To be attractive, we need to stop pretending we are someone else.

Physical beauty is overrated in our world. Therefore, we think that everyone looking good is a nice person, and we attribute positive personality traits to physically attractive people. In time, we accumulate enough people experience to become aware that our expectations are not always correct. We begin to understand that attraction is not only about physical beauty. Being genuinely attractive is about knowing your inner light and expressing it through the harmony of your desires, values, and goals.

Here are a few important messages about attraction you can share with your daughter:

Self-confidence is at the core of attractiveness. People that are sure of themselves fascinate others and peck their interest. Make sure that your daughter can make the difference between true self-belief, and pride and pretentiousness.

Healthy self-confidence includes acceptance of our good traits, as well as awareness of our shortcomings. Such a person is usually aware of the weaknesses and is trying to self-improve. On the other hand, our self-confidence depends on our core qualities. Our core self should be built of an ample dose of self-respect and self-acceptance, and of a specific modesty that enables staying close to others. The secret of the self-confidence is in maintaining a harmony of these characteristics.

Tell your daughter to be herself. Being unique and incomparable is an advantage. In a world of copycat personalities and so much similar taste, to stand out, a young woman needs to be able to keep her essence. We are often in fear that expressive individuality can take us into social isolation, encourage critique and result in ostracizing.

In the teen age, in particular, a big nose, a weight that is not ideal, a disproportionate face, or a tall or short body can become serious impediments to your daughter's attractiveness, and can negatively affect her self-confidence. As a result, she starts believing that with such physical qualities she is unable to attract the interest of others for real. She becomes suspicious of her own qualities. Help her avoid this by teaching her to fall in love with her uniqueness and her irreplaceable visceral world.

Many secrets of attraction are hidden in the body language. It all starts with how we look at others. We should know how to establish eye contact. If we are aware of how we treat our body in the environment, we will notice when we cross our arms and legs. As much as they can become ingrown habits, crossing arms and legs are critical obstacles to gaining other people's trust.

This doesn't mean that if your daughter feels uncomfortable around someone, she should welcome him or her with open arms. Yet we shouldn't underestimate the power of our hands and head gestures, as well as the power of our smile. They can touch on another person's interest, evoke trust and create closeness.

When we express closeness, know how to listen to others and communicate with empathy, we get more and more attractive to others. If we talk only about ourselves and about our best qualities, skills, and abilities, we create unpleasant scenarios and a distance that's difficult to bridge.

All of us should learn how to create intimacy. If you want to be attractive, you should know how to put your identity out there, be genuinely interested in what the other person has to say and stop acting toward others in a pompous way.

Talk to your daughter about finding something original about herself. Let her challenge the social norms. A woman who is fully compliant with what the society has to say, adhering to its standards and taste, is slowly becoming a meaningless drop in the sea of mediocrity. Of course, there is no originality when this happens!

If she wants to attract some attention and a few glances in a crowd, she should find a detail that helps her stand out in the vast sea of average. Thanks to her one-of-a-kind quirkiness, she will make an impression and attract people's attention. People would be interested to find out more about that.

Without a doubt, her originality should be in accordance with her looks and her internal self. Pretending and adopting someone else's image won't bear any fruit. On the contrary, it will take her away from her own nature and produce the opposite effect.

As your daughter gets older, it will become her habit to gain new insights into these concepts. They grow with experience and enhanced self-knowledge.

Simply put, only when we have a thorough understanding of who we are, we get an idea of the sides of our character we should develop. We get to know our strengths and how they are born with the magic that attracts other people's attention to our personality.

Chapter 12

The Pleasure and Luxury of Growing Old as a Woman

There is something very unique to every woman - the ability to give birth, create and nurture herself and others through her menstrual cyclical nature. Your daughter's jump into the teenage years and adolescence is marked by her menarche and will affect many of the processes and the difficult conversations you are going to touch during this period.

In a similar way as with many other female-related subjects, we are not totally in tune with the benefits of our menstrual cycles and how to use them in building better lives for ourselves. Menstruation has hidden messages that can help us improve our decision-making skills in many areas.

In contrast to the beneficial nature of the menstrual cycle, the popular opinion is that periods are still a problem - something that makes our living difficult, and not something that could be used as guidance. Very often, periods are considered shameful and disgusting. This attitude is tightly woven into the overall picture of women's bodies and sexual nature.

Puberty is the best time to share positive messages about menstruation with your daughter. Hopefully, you have done most of the legwork on the subject before. In case you haven't, these years are the perfect time for your daughter to understand how to get in tune with her changing body, what happens during the cycle and why she should consider the menstrual cycle a privilege and a luxury. It will help her acknowledge the cycles and the seasons in nature, as well as stay in touch with her own nature. It will help her gain a perspective of time and a wholesome picture of woman's life all the way to growing old.

Above all, let your daughter know that periods are the perfect moment for rest, creativity and getting in touch with her core self. Bleeding is a time for a huge personal space and basking in luxury.

Luxury means so very different things to so many women, but in the age of informational distraction, achievement pressure and less time for the creative void, she should take a couple of days for herself as a basic luxury.

Let her period remind her to nourish her body and soul because that's when we most need some TLC, and we easily forget to give it to ourselves. If there is time to do this every month, there are fewer chances to worry, stress and obsess about irrelevant issues.

Luxury often means stopping the duty treadmill and taking the time to pause. It's not always about expensive stuff. However, this often turns out to be the biggest challenge for women, especially when they juggle tasks or multiple duties.

Let your daughter dedicate some self-care each month. This habit will help her ride the waves of changing hormones as she grows older, all the way to menopause. The small luxury of time taken each month will influence her flourishing later during menopause. Because this is the time that our bodies tax us for our lifelong habits, these 'me-times' will be precious investments that will produce lifelong dividends. The habit of self-care during menstruation will help her make the right choices and avoid rushing through life by automatism.

Chapter 13

How to Talk About Sexuality

Why an Early Chat about Consent is Worth its Weight in Gold

Dedicating time to talk to your daughter about consent before she becomes a teenager will save you a whole lot of effort once she passes a certain age. It's good to start teaching consent even when she is very young. For example, bath time when your girl is younger is an excellent moment to explain consent; by letting your daughter choose the body parts she wants to wash by herself, she decides upon her own level of comfort with physical touch.

Physical affection is a subject that permeates family relationships with cousins. Many people consider physical affection a rule. However, that's not how things should always be. It's best to discuss consent even for yourself, as a mom.

Your daughter doesn't "owe" a hug, a handshake or a kiss to anyone. Yes, that includes you, too! Telling her that she should show physical affection only because the other person is a relative, or because she or he has been away for a while, or because it is a special occasion, means that she will disconnect from her genuine need. She will start manipulating physical affection or trading with it once she grows into an adult.

Doctor exams are another good place to talk about consent. The likelihood of her having her first ob-gyn check when she is a teenager is high; she shouldn't be uncomfortable about saying no, ever. Tell her that she has the right to know what will happen at the exam and agree to every part of it.

Starting young with consent saves her from adopting an unhealthy pattern down the road. Boundaries should be respected at all times. Otherwise, kisses and hugs as a child can translate into sexual activities once your daughter becomes a teenager. Tell her that she doesn't have to be "nice" by displaying physical affection. She can choose her own way of being polite and courteous. She can write a thank you note, smile or just simply nod or say "Thank you". While politeness is a sign of good social manners, she doesn't owe anyone affection.

The load of affection put on little girls and young women turns into emotional labor for adults. Emotional labor means emotional management according to the requirements or the expectations of others. While we as social creatures do this sometimes, becoming too affectionate can often include carrying unpleasant emotions for others and getting emotionally drained as a result.

Some believe that strict consent rules and depriving your daughter of physical touch can mean growing a person with a low tolerance for closeness and intimacy. That might be true. Let them be. What works for others might not work for them. Give your daughter space to decide what the right distance between her and other people is. No one can know but her.

Talking About Sex and Pleasure

As I am writing this book, it's 2018 and we are in a midst of media frenzy over disclosed sexual harassment cases that were long hidden behind a smokescreen. For some, these revelations were difficult to swallow. That's normal; there is always some resistance to digest gut-wrenching truths.

In all that darkness, we've forgotten that sex is a pleasurable activity. While you are talking your daughter about consent, and what it means to respect her body boundaries, don't forget to mention that sex is a good thing, too. Pleasure and consent are very much connected. Feeling bad or uncomfortable about sexual contact should make your daughter aware that boundaries have been crossed.

Sexual assault is bad. Horrible. But sex is good.

Consider this message as a part of a homeschooling sex-ed class. Sexuality and pleasure are beautiful. When done right, they form the base of the closest and most intimate loving contact. What's wrong with sex is the abuse of power in sexual relationships. What's amazing about sex is people who enjoy reciprocal, consensual and pleasurable contact.

The Force of Life: Sexuality as a Creative Energy

Sexuality is vitality. By channeling sexuality and reproduction, we bring new people to life on this planet. Channeled sexuality is the quill pen of beautiful literature. It's the brush of a painter's masterpiece and the musical instrument of a first-class composer.

Sexuality is related to divinity. Institutionalized religions are in deep denial of the connection between divine beings and sexuality. We can interpret this process as purposeful and as a control measure or as an unconscious attitude shaped by unresolved collective shadow processes. It is a matter of perspective and both reasons can be considered as different sides of the same story. You can give the vibrating life force a name of a deity or you can call it sexual energy. In both cases, its existence is unquestionable.

The purpose of this extraordinary energy is not to control, demean, shame, posses or engage in power-plays with another. When we disconnect from the affirming quality of sex, we are easily exploitable by social constructs about sex.

Why is this important to keep in mind when your daughter is a teenager? If she is able to talk to you about complex issues, she will consider you her best ally. Normally, not all aspects of sexuality should be discussed as early as thirteen. Some, like this interpretation of sexuality, are more appropriate at the end of adolescence.

How can you talk to your daughter about finding her place in a sex-slandering culture, in which the shame in view of pleasure is supporting the abuse of power? Is there a way to develop a healthy view of a deeply intimate subject with a lot of wounding on a personal and collective level? How can your daughter be sensitive to her own needs for pleasure while respecting the boundaries of another? How can she ask for the same in return?

Here is a guide she can use to address confusion in sexually intimate relationships. While not all questions can be answered at once, approaching them with this basic knowledge can turn her loving relationships into beautiful spaces for contact, connection, and deep respect.

Brief History of Female Sexual Pleasure

Nowadays, we are used to seeing pleasure as an inseparable part of sex. The history of sexual pleasure, though, is somewhat different to how we connect to sex and pleasure today. In the past, women's connection to pleasure was not always important. Sometimes, it was even secondary or non-existent. In as much as we want to see the current situation differently, there are remnants from the past even now.

A hundred years ago, the popular role of women in sex was more about reproduction then it was about sex. The reason for the sex's existence was to create new life. Moral sex was connected with family and reproduction. The immoral sex was connected with pleasure. No one actually thought that women could never feel pleasure, but the general opinion that was pushed in the public agenda was that women's bodies need to bear new lives for political, social and cultural reasons. One legitimate reason, as many believed so, was for the growth of a nation.

Female pleasure was closely tied to the role of the mother or the wife. It was extracted from the role of the woman as a lover capable of pleasure outside of the marriage and the family. Women who really enjoyed sex were not considered the mainstream model. Some of them were even treated as unnatural.

Aside from the political and cultural factors, the absence of female pleasure was also due to practical reasons. The non-existence of modern birth control made it difficult for women to indulge in sexual pleasure. Pregnancy fear is famous to curb one's desire. In history, it affected the role of women as erotic lovers. Although there were out-of-the-blue marriages, which means that sex before marriage was practiced, most unmarried and married women suffered from the fear of an unwanted child.

This was a big reason for women to stay away from sex, regardless of the ever-present sexual desire. Women in individual cases knew how to find sex for pleasure only, but the general concept of enjoyment and orgasm was rarely mentioned. Out of the bounds of marriage, passionate and desirous women were not seen that often.

This split of sexless youth and sexually active marriages created not only problems in women's lives, but it also distorted relationships. For men, on the contrary, the widely accepted opinion was that they should feel desire and pleasure all the time. From cold and desire-free non-married life, a girl was expected to suddenly start enjoying marriage "duties". Connecting sex with duty influenced pleasure. There isn't much pleasure in obligations, right?

While this was the situation in the early 20th century, the years that led to the next few decades started changing this conventional view of sex, pleasure, and marriage. Romance took a different turn, including more flirting and erotic play, and more frequent sex for pleasure. It was the age before the Second World War and freedom was seen in a new way.

(It is important to make the difference between this period and the years after the war to understand how society affects our most intimate lives. Such deeper understanding creates some detachment from cultural constraints. It will help your daughter live a fulfilled life where she finds her own voice of pleasure among the plethora of opinions around her.)

The years after the war reversed the trend. Women took the conservative 'virginal' role before marriage again and were expected to adopt the sexual pleasure split - sexless girls, and sexual brides and wives. In marriage, women were expected to enjoy sex. Any discrepancy between reality and the expectations was seen as some sort of disorder. A pleasureless woman became a big marital problem.

 In the next few decades, birth control, especially the pill, shifted these attitudes in the opposite way. Just in time, women got hold of an accessible means of birth control, along with popular movements for freedom, the emergence of anti-war communities and changing the social landscape of sexuality. The social liberalism affected the sexual revolutions around the world. The pill made space for more pleasure to enter into women's lives, removing the fear of pregnancy and making sex available outside of the reproductive marital restraints. In fact, sexual pleasure started becoming the main component of sex, without its mandatory attachment to legally binding relationships.

In a hundred years, social roles for girls and women were rapidly changing in line with what was happening in society. If we expand this short sexual history to several hundred or even to several thousand years back, we will clarify the importance of social factors with certainty.

Making allowance for views of female sexual pleasure that are outside of the current western civilization adds significant leeway on how we shape our attitudes toward sexuality. Acknowledging that female (and male) bodies are conditioned by social expectations will be precious for your daughter to gain self-confidence in her sexuality and develop an intuitive bodily understanding.

How are things as we speak? The ideas of female sexual pleasure are still complicated. Girls are expected to adhere to wildly different opinions. There is a constant open discussion about how young women should behave. Social media makes things for teenage girls even more complex: on one hand, they need to be sexy and attractive, but not openly, passionately or aggressively sexual; on the other hand, there are often hit with the social slaps of morality, slut-shaming, and rape culture.

(Rape culture is not an overly discussed topic in this book, but that doesn't mean that it is not one of the difficult conversations you will, at some point, going to have with your daughter. There is so much heated discussion in the media. Excluding it from this book is to avoid suffocation with overwhelmingly popular subjects and pay due attention to other important topics for teenage girls. You will, however, find interrelated threads of rape culture with some of the other topics in this book.)

A Tough Nut to Break: Porn, Drugs, and Alcohol

Controversial topics such as porn, drugs, and alcohol evoke strong feelings with many parents. As a mother, you can get all anxious when you need to touch upon the subject with your teenage daughter, especially if you have stayed away from the topics for a long time and you are now getting some tough questions.

While there is so much information about drugs and alcohol online, porn is pretty controversial. Most parents don't really feel confident and comfortable about breaking the idea of talking about it with their adolescents. Most of the approaches related to talking about porn that will be discussed here apply to drugs and alcohol, too, so feel free to adapt them. But, porn is a really tricky subject - no wonder so many get disturbed about the lack of and the misinformation about it.

Most moms think that availability of porn on the Internet is an issue. Yet, porn is rarely discussed, and not many parents know how to find good resources. It is therefore important to prepare yourself when you speak about porn.

A good place to start is to get personally informed about porn so that you know where you come from and what your standpoint is. Grown-ups typically have an array of negative feelings about porn, such as shame, disgust or fear. Coming from that viewpoint doesn't make difficult conversations any easier. If anything, it makes them more difficult.

What can you do to help yourself?

Sharing your concern, fear, and shame around the topic with other moms can help you relieve some of the anxiety and worry you have so that you are able to approach the conversation with your daughter with warmth, self-assurance, and in a relaxed and non-judgmental way.

Moms (and parents overall!) often use scare tactics to warn children against sex, drugs or alcohol. These seldom work. Catastrophic consequences that accompany the scare tactics are rarely based on true knowledge. When you are trying to scare your daughter with information that is not true, and she is seeing that other children are going through the same without ending up dead or hurt, you will not only lose your integrity as a parent, but you can also make your way into an unreliable, scared and an unsafe source of information. That's not where a mom wants to be.

Why Scare Tactics Can Be Counterintuitive

Overwhelmed by the role of protectors, moms can jump straight to scaremongering and destruct the safe container they are building for their daughters. You want to be the trusted ally for your daughter and to keep communication channels open. If you are only moralizing, without supporting your claims with authoritative information, your daughter will turn to other resources to learn the truth.

With so much damaging and false information on the Internet, you want to be the safe haven for guidance and active help for your daughter, whenever she encounters difficulties about these topics in life. She should be able to breach the topic with you at any time.

Porn is typically associated with fear, shame, confusion, and worry. This is why it's smart to get rid of the drama of these feelings when you need to discuss them with your daughter. Preparation is key, and when done in groups with other moms, it is so much easier. These groups can serve to discuss a number of controversial topics in a non-shaming way and to address other issues about puberty and sexuality, and drugs and alcohol. Overall, talking about porn will be easier if you do your own work around it.

Porn is omnipresent. It's good to preach some aspects of it when a girl is younger because if she doesn't hear it from her mom, she will hear it at school, in the neighborhood or find it on the web. Smartphones are everywhere. Sometimes, even they needn't be included.

I remember my first experience with porn. At that time, I had no idea it was porn and didn't quite understand the meaning of what I saw, perhaps only vaguely. The event was about a few pages torn from a magazine; movies were not that accessible in that period. It came to my possession by accident, when a nosey friend discovered them in her older brother's room. I was around ten, and this was a couple of decades ago.

Therefore, we need to be aware that very young children can gain access to a smartphone and see porn. And this is a good point to make when you are talking to your daughter about such a sensitive topic - she shouldn't feel that she must watch what someone else is showing her on a smartphone. Saying no to this is important for accentuating decision-making skills and making strong choices in a very delicate area.

Obviously, not all questions should be discussed all at once, but the following paragraphs can serve you as an ideation process of what might come up from your teenage (or younger) daughter.

Pornography is not about real sex. The porn industry is about profits. Some types of porn with a nuance of erotica are more acceptable for some people. From personal worldviews, it's difficult to make a strict distinction between genres. Many people find reading erotica or watching porn exciting, refreshing and stimulating. However, if you only associate sex with the mainstream porn where most of the scenes include degradation, humiliation, and violence, you won't be able to make the distinction between a movie performance and real sex.

It's important that your daughter knows that porn is a fantasy. Some people do have sex like presented in porn, but not all sex is like that. Sex can be weird, strange, loving and intimate. Porn is a performance marathon. There is a spectrum of feelings associated with real-life sex, which porn lacks. Partners in real sex experience a full range of emotions that can range from ecstasy to sadness. They are vulnerable and intimate. It's important to make the point that mutuality, vulnerability, and closeness are an inevitable part of real sex. The perception of sex should not be painted by porn.

Talk about porn stars and the image they are trying to portray on film. Female porn stars are like dolls. They are styled, filtered, staged and directed. Many are even surgically altered. Your daughter should not expect to look like that; neither should she have certain expectations from male partners.

If you have waited to talk to your teenage daughter about consent for too long, some of the difficult conversations around porn will be even more demanding. For example, porn often includes non-consensual sex. If you haven't talked about consent, let her know that real sex with consent is about active participation, consciousness, and enthusiasm along the way.

In real sex, you don't care about the performance. You care that the other person is equally engaged in whatever you are doing. Continuity in consent means that any participant can change their mind along the way. Consent is not given once and for all. Learning about boundaries with touching, hugging and kissing as a small child would have definitely helped your daughter distinguish between consensual sex with and sex without consent.

Girls need to be raised with the message that their pleasure matters and that their engagement in sex is not to be of service. Maybe the best way to affirm women's pleasure during sex is to support self-pleasure. Self-pleasuring is wonderful. Girls need to hear that sexual pleasure is good and that feeling good about their bodies is healthy. Being able to feel pleasure is a part of the body's intuitive focus. What feels good about the body can help teenage (and younger) girls understand more about their own pleasure.

Pleasure is nurturing and important for our growth. Many small children are curious about sex and they start playing with their bodies even when they are very young. Such activities should be supported and affirmed, but they should be done in private and behind closed doors.

When your daughter is a bit older, you can initiate more conversations about sexuality. Children aged 8 or 9 find great use in books about puberty. This is a great way to normalize all changes in puberty and one of the best tools to help you deal with your own nervousness, anxiety, and shame with these topics.

Many illustrated books depict straightforward and accurate descriptions of puberty and what it means for the body. This age may be appropriate to mention condoms in a fun way and talk about their role in birth control and STDs. The strategy of condom bowls (putting a bunch of condoms into the open when the girl gets 15 or 16 years old) works better than expected.

Making condoms visible is not an act of sex encouragement. It's about keeping the lines of communications open and about letting your daughter know that you are there for her to support her in any way you can.

In the end, mention that porn is not the best sex-ed tool. Girls should not rely on porn to get their sex ed basics. Watching too much porn stimulates and trains the brain to get used to porn images. This conversation may not be convenient for younger girls because of the scare tactics, but girls aged thirteen need to hear that. It's always better to hear the information from a mom than struggle with misinformation from unreliable sources.

One critical message about porn your daughter needs to hear is about porn and shaming.

If you watch porn, you are not a bad person. Your daughter's view of porn should be free of shame and led by her personal choices supported by her mom's non-judgmental guidance.

Grown-ups also watch porn, many parents do, and we wouldn't want the girls to think that their parents are bad persons. Shame and porn don't go together well. At this point, you can clarify that not all porn stars are exploited, do porn only because of economic desperation or feel that porn devalues them as individuals. On the contrary, many find pleasure and empowerment in the job they do. Although a large number of porn stars are treated poorly, aren't allowed to use condoms, must work for long hours and don't get to choose the sexual acts they get into, many are happy with what they do. Do not paint the absolute negative picture of porn stars.

However, porn's mainstream message is not about loving our bodies. It is about meeting external standards, making other people happy and using our bodies as commodities for someone else's benefit. You can stay away from your inner drama while discussing this, share your personal feelings, but let your daughter make her own choices.

Chapter 14

Motherhood & Parenting - Why It Is More about the Hows than the Whys

No mother is the same, yet - they are all alike. Even when moms agree with this statement, the concept of motherhood is not the same for everyone. There is no simple, one right way to be a mom.

Your daughter will learn about what motherhood is from your own example. You can talk as much as you like, but if you don't support your talk with action, it's the action that will prevail and set the example. That doesn't mean that your daughter won't be interested in what it means to be a good mother. She may even become one as young as a teenager.

Be prepared to answer some difficult questions about motherhood from your daughter. More or less, she will challenge her role model - you. When she wants to breach the subject, you can use a framework that will help you answer difficult questions, navigate your own way through your daughter's teen age and make decisions by using it as guidance.

"How come you know you are a good mother and that you make the right decisions?", your daughter may ask.

Great question!

What is a good mother? Or - what is a good parent?

Building a Motherhood Framework

Most of this book will give you enough material to crystallize a few of your own motherhood truths. If your daughter wants to find her own voice in how she wants to be a mom, that is totally fine. But in case she wants to turn over to you, here is a summary of important principles that can serve this purpose:

Keep your daughter active in the family power balance. To make the best decisions, think of the children, the parents, and the family as partners with equal stakes in needs.

Use self-reflection as your first tool. Instead of making it all about the children, why don't you investigate your own triggers and see if some issues are actually more about yourself?

Love leads the way. Leave fear, anger, and resentment aside when you make the decisions. It's hard to be a parent. Choose to mother with love, patience, forethought, and intuition.

Follow with respect. They may be young, but children are nonetheless persons. Respect their personality as you would do for a grown-up.

Focus on growth, ditch control. Grownups like a quiet, clean and organized house. When growing, children find a million ways to mess this order up. Make sure that you let your child do this. Don't control everything.

Children are awesome teachers. Every child possesses an inner wisdom that somehow gets lost on the way up to adulthood. Pick up these wisdom treasures and treat them gently.

Stay flexible. Check, double-check and be prepared to rethink and rewrite your parenting strategy. What we believe will work, turns into a sour solution. Knowing that the time for a new approach has come is a gem of parenting.

Rectifying Common Talking and Parenting Mistakes

The relationship between a mother and a daughter is one of the most serious relationships in the life of every woman. The way a mother behaves toward her young daughter on her journey to growing up affects her future destiny. Consequently, the parenting role is painful for many parents. What are the most common mistakes mothers (and parents) communicate to their daughters?

Not Leading by Example

Instead of telling your daughter: "You have to learn how to cook", you can say - "Let's make this delicious salad together". Then, follow through with action. When a girl sees that her mom is happy to do something, she will also be eager to learn the skills.

Condemning Sex

If your girl listened to the same attitude about sex since she was a child (that men want only one thing) she will grow up with the opinion that all men are thugs, and that sex is a disgusting activity. There is a fundamental paradox in the statement that sex is a dirty thing, but that your daughter needs to get married and have a child, preferably by a certain age. The result of setting conflicting beliefs is making her frightened of relationships altogether.

Smothering and Over-Caring

If you care too much, your daughter can grow up with a deformed personality with no personal opinions. There is a greater danger that she will be manipulated by the environment.

A Negative Fatherly Model

If you keep telling your daughter that her father is a fool, the girl will start feeling guilty that she has that man for a father. With this feeling of guilt, she will aim to accommodate everyone and prove herself because she won't be able to cope with the negative model of her father's heritage.

Physical Violence

Corporal punishment is humiliating for girls, maybe even more than it is for boys. If a girl gets physically punished, she will start adopting a victim behavior and choose aggressive partners. Quarreling in front of a child is a hard knock on its mental health. Don't forget that a child often takes responsibility for what is happening in the family.

Lack of Praise and Communication

Growing without praise ends up in a self-loveless life. Your daughter will turn into a grown person that won't be able to act as an equal partner in relationships. If you don't talk to your daughter and avoid answering her "stupid" questions, especially during adolescence, she will lose the connection with you and feel abandoned. Think of it in this way: there is never a limit to the time you can talk to your daughter and answer her countless questions - the more you do it, the better.

A Distorted View of Life

Don't tell your daughter that she should live her life according to a predetermined set of rules. There are no mandatory ingredients for a happy and successful life, and the list most certainly doesn't always include marriage, children, a specific profession or having the right weight. She should know that she has the right to do whatever she chooses and pleases. This is the only way to bring about a healthy and happy womanhood for your teenage daughter.

During her life, she will hear many conflicting messages. Coming to the personal truth in the multivocal environment is not easy - this is where you come to direct her toward finding her own voice in the world. If you respect her individual opinion, you are on a great way to support her in questioning the voices around her.

Chapter 15

Messages Your Daughter Should Question at All Times

There is no right way for the toys a girl should use. Dolls and kitchens are as good as cars and trucks.

The media is not always the right place to choose role-models, especially if you are looking for a female role model, simply for the reason, there aren't many.

School dress codes are questionable. You are not responsible for how the way you are dressed affects another person's perception or behavior. Don't succumb to body-shaming, slut-shaming and age shaming, regardless of the side you are on - don't slut-shame, body-shame or age-shame.

Periods. They are neither disgusting nor a nuisance. They are a way your body works together with nature to channel an amazing creative energy that makes babies and the most beautiful creations in the world, including art.

Virginity. Do you really need to protect a social construct? There are various misconceptions about virginity, not only social but also anatomical. Find out how your body is really built before you believe mainstream media and educators with an agenda.

There is a lack of sexual education in our schools and that's a problem. Teenage pregnancies are not the same everywhere in the world. Sexual education has a lot to do with it. Abstinence is not the best solution. Question the birth control you can use. Ask for its accessibility. Birth control is not only your responsibility as a woman.

Your sexuality is natural and beautiful. It's alright to be confused about it.

Bullying and harassment are unacceptable - from men and from women.

Science, technology, engineering, and mathematics are not only the boys' choice of education and career. Sports is not only for boys.

There is not a specific way your body should look like. You don't need to get married by a certain age or ever if you don't want to. You don't need to have children if you don't want to.

In pregnancy, you carry a new life. As much as a new life is your personal responsibility as a mom, you need support from your family and society. While your body will usually carry the baby, when you are pregnant you should be "carried" by your container, because bringing new lives into existence requires community support. Continually question and challenge medical advice around pregnancy and infertility.

Abortion is your right. The choice can be as devastating as it can be. You don't need someone else to make the procedure worse by patronizing, moralizing or telling you lies about what you can and can't do with your body.

Divorce laws, domestic violence laws, employment laws, and maternity laws are not perfect. Question your rights and responsibilities. Initiate a change when necessary.

Absence is often more important, but more difficult to notice than presence. Think of female leadership and the absence of it on the social scene.

Motherhood. You don't need to be a stay-at-home mom. You don't need to be a go-to-work mom. You don't have to be a career mom. You don't need to forget about going to work once you become a mom. Breastfeeding in public or in private is your choice.

International women problems are real and they show their ugly faces even in the most advanced or civilized societies. Female infanticide, genital mutilation, forced marriages, and child brides, honor killings and sex trafficking are painful, but you need to be aware of them.

(The teenage years spreads over a longer course. It's definitely better to bring some of these difficult issues into the open when your daughter is at the end of this period. Yet it is also wise to stay prepared and think of an age-appropriate discussion around the topics. In the end, you

never know when she will come across such an issue and start asking questions).

Three Gifts to Give to Your Daughter (When You Don't Have the Time for Reading Books)

If you want to take just three critical messages from this book, then choose the following:

Help your daughter build the confidence to know her self-worth.

Let her develop the strength to chase her dreams

Never let her doubt how deeply, truly loved she is.

I bet any mom would agree!

From a Daughter Who Doesn't Mind Speaking about Difficult Topics (Author's Note)

I grew up as a daughter of parents who didn't mind talking about many difficult topics. They took a no-nonsense approach, and I am forever grateful for the ways they used when discussing unpleasant subjects.

Instead of lying or manipulating the truth they choose to explain things in the manner I could understand. I think that was a blessing! It makes me happy and prideful in how mature I seem to be today. Although, if you ask them,

I'm sure that they will find plenty of material to find faults in the job they did or in the way I turned up!

In spite of trying to do the best job they could, no parents are perfect. They weren't ready or just didn't have the skills or the knowledge about how important it's to speak about certain topics. I wish I could have received some messages differently. I wish there was more information publicly available as I grew up. As a blessing or as a curse, the Internet didn't exist then, so I had to educate myself from books and magazines.

Most of the messages in this book are those that I wish I would have received when I was a teenager. Of course, not all of them will be appropriate for your situation. And not all of them will go well with all ages; so a little discernment is necessary for finding the right moment to talk about them with your daughter.

The book is not intended to be medical or professional advice from experts. It is a story of a daughter who decided to share some knowledge from the personal library of resources collected over years of bookworming, workshops, professional education, and life experience. If you have troubles talking to a teenager, give yourself a small pat on the back - you are facing someone who defies authority by the nature of things. You definitely need some special skills. If you find them here, this book has served its purpose. If you don't, you'll at least acknowledge that you are not alone in your role as a mom. Again, this book has somewhat served its purpose.

Good luck!

One last thing!

I want to give you a **one-in-two-hundred chance** to win a **$200.00 Amazon Gift card** as a thank-you for reading this book.

All I ask is that you give me some feedback, so I can improve this or my next book :)

Your opinion is *super valuable* to me. It will only take a minute of your time to let me know what you like and what you didn't like about this book. The hardest part is deciding how to spend the two hundred dollars! Just follow this link.

http://reviewers.win/momdaughter

About the Author

Biljana Ognenova is a passionate and an intuitive writer with a background in law and psychology, and over 15 years of experience in management of people and projects in an international environment. She invests a lot of her spare time to master psychology at work, especially topics about teams in organizations, organizational justice, and employee well-being. Biljana has completed hundreds of hours in Gestalt group psychotherapy training and attended dozens of workshops related to communication and conflict in groups. She also has a certificate for mentoring girls and facilitating Girls' Circles from the 'Journey of Young Women' and is looking to spread a positive message for girls' empowerment and coming of age. While finishing her postgraduate studies in psychology, Biljana is building a well-rounded writing portfolio by crafting beautiful stories for special people.

Made in the USA
Coppell, TX
08 January 2025

44132375R00059